Within the Classroom; Past Tense Verbs

Copyright, Revised Edition

This product may be copied for the purchaser's class only.

It breaks copyright law to share, swap or re-sell this product.

By Mary Meyers

ISBN 978-1-927704-05-9

Illegal use of this copyright resource includes swapping, sharing or resale.

The purchaser of this book may reproduce this book for only his/her class instruction.

Referencing the author is required when using any part of this book for staff PD or other teacher-training.

Copyright 2019
Mary Meyers

Attention Teachers

There are no page numbers.

This sequence is not rigid.

Use any activities at any time when they meet the needs of your students.

Use any event as a teaching event; birthdays, trips, holiday vocabulary.

Newcomers may arrive at any time of year - you'll always have the basics.

Thinking and Talking are work.
Laughter is a form of communication.

Table of Contents

Why Verb Words?
English Verb Tenses
Teaching Grammar
Teaching Basic Verbs
Why Bingo?
Magazine Verb Books
Verb Worksheets
More Verbs – Past Tense
Past Tense –ed Endings
Past Tense Practice Worksheets
Helping Verbs
Future Tense Forms
Infinitives and Gerunds
Brainstorming
Change a Word Game
Adverbs
Two-Word Verbs
Culture
Continuous Past Tense
Location Verbs
Surveys, Polls, Questionnaires and Interviews
What do you lile to do? Hobbies
Jobs
Perfect is a Tense
Verb Comprehension, Cognition and Equity
Verbs as Cognitive Processes
Worksheets
Thesaurus
Idioms
Teaching Verbs Article

Why Verb Words ?

In large part, the words chosen for this book are based on the verb words for beginning readers. 'High-frequency' word lists can be found on the Internet; the Dolch list for beginning readers along with other high frequency lists. These verb words are considered to be grade 1 'sight' words for beginning reading; children are supposed to be able to read or recognize each word on sight, based on the configuration of letters and/or from the context when it was presented.

Concrete nouns are the easiest words to learn to read since they represent real and concrete objects. Abstract words are harder to learn since it's not as easy to draw a picture or to touch them. i.e., put, want, need, must

The choice of verbs in this teacher reproducible book rely, as well, on the vocabulary for beginning speakers of English. Pages should be enlarged when working with primary students since students should print the word in each box.

Introduce each word in print and oral context simultaneously.

To review the word for reading and comprehension, ask primary students to print it on the computer in different fonts, and after to draw one favorite context for a class-made book. Older students ought to compose sentences with the teacher, copy them down and then print them on the computer.

English Verb Tenses

Present Tenses

1. Simple Present - He <u>watches</u> sports on TV.
2. Present Continuous - He <u>is watching</u> sports on TV.
3. Present Perfect - He <u>has watched</u> sports on TV every night.
4. Present Perfect Continuous - He <u>has been watching</u> sports on TV all day.

> **Note:**
> Continuous tenses always use the basic verb plus - ing.
> Perfect tenses always use have or had.

Past Tenses

1. Simple Past - He <u>watched</u> sports on TV.
2. Past Continuous - He <u>was watching</u> sports on TV.
3. Past Perfect - He <u>had watched</u> sports on TV instead of playing the sport.
4. Present Perfect Continuous - He <u>had been watching</u> sports on TV when it broke.

Future Tenses

1. Simple Future - He <u>will watch</u> sports on TV. (indicating an intention or promise)
   - He <u>is going to watch</u> TV. (indicates a plan or inevitability)
2. Future Continuous - He will be watching sports on TV.
3. Future Perfect - He <u>will have watched</u> sports on TV every night.
   - (This tense refers to the past.)
4. Future Perfect Continuous - He <u>will have been watching</u> sports on TV.

> Conditionals - could, would, should - I <u>would watch</u> TV if sports were on.
> Modals - helping verbs such as can, may, might, ought to, etc.

Verb Knowledge and Tense

English language learners beyond the level of basic, interpersonal fluency will know a limited range of verbs, certain past tenses and probably one way of forming the future tense - "will". This section will provide ideas for teaching and reviewing essential verb vocabulary.

- *use verbs from a reading selection in riddles, spelling lists, cloze passages, games, definitions, BINGO and word searches*

- *brainstorming of nouns, verbs, adjectives on your topic*

- *use Readers' Theatre*

- *dramatize events or character parts from the text*

- *require thesaurus or dictionary work for specific verbs from the reading selection or text*

- *access bilingual dictionaries for student use in classes*

Past Tense Paranoia

This title is not just meant to get your attention. Irregular past tense verbs are the most difficult to learn. In fact, even students from English-speaking homes could do with a thorough review, along with spelling tests. Besides worksheets for learning past tense verb forms, students could do activities such as cut and paste bright magazine verbs, label and put in alphabetical order for a class book, BINGO, write "Mad Libs", play charades or mime, etc.

Teaching Grammar, Parts of Speech and Verb Tenses

English Language Learners/ELLs from grade 3 up benefit from explicit, targeted instruction concerning the Parts of Speech in English. Older students will already have a sense of 'grammar' from their native language although they may not be able to state the rules or to name of the parts of speech.

Even primary-age students should learn about nouns, adjectives, verbs, pronouns, adverbs, prepositions and joining words or cohesive devices; the instruction and activities however ought to be age-appropriate and include simplified concepts without reams of worksheet exercises. Primary teachers can use class lists, magazine cut-outs, brainstorming (all the nouns in the classroom) matching games, computer programs as well as posters. Instruction will frame student knowledge of sentence formation and serve as a base for future learning of phrases, complex sentences and clauses.

Students should learn to identify past, present and future tenses of verbs. They ought to learn to recognize various formations of a root word verb and irregular past tenses.

Educators of English Language Learners ELLs

Students are NOT meant to work alone on these skill pages. Teachers ought to consider the worksheets as instructional guides in helping students learn a particular concept with its related vocabulary and tasks.

Skills are introduced in a simple clear fashion and directions and tasks are well spaced and easy to follow.

ELL students benefit from hearing the intonation and clear enunciation of vocabulary modeled by their teacher. Older students will not usually need much more information once the concept/skill is introduced. If younger students require extra practice, there are many activities available from grade-level teachers and on the internet.

The concepts and vocabulary can be reviewed the next day, but as always lessons ought to focus on speech as a tool for literacy.

Teaching with a Whiteboard

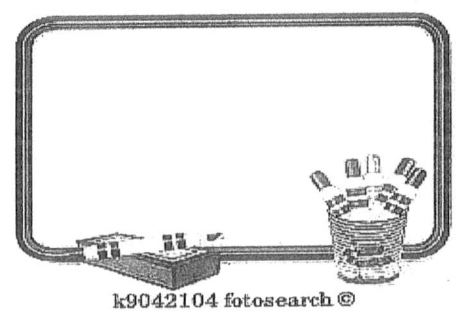

Make a clean copy of a topic picture page or review activity, scan it and add it as a new file on your computer.

Create a Whiteboard folder and move the teaching sheet to it.

When you are presenting new vocabulary, move the file onto the whiteboard and the screen. Students will see it better and you will be able to focus student attention and learning better.

- You can also use it to label pictures/write in answers as students copy it onto their own paper copy.

- Review the vocabulary. Use a 'say it and point to it' activity using a single word, a riddle, a category, or a context phrase or sentence. i.e., pencil, yellow pencil, Where is my yellow pencil? What can you write with?

The activity also models the way that partners can play at their desks, which is a good way to practise for listening and speaking.

Verb

A word that is an action.

TEACHING BASIC VERBS

The following picture pages will assist you to introduce or review many basic verbs in either the present or the past tenses.

Use the verb pictures;

* to name and spell (label) each verb action
* get a translation from student's bilingual dictionary
* copy to make a matching or memory game
* make a set of flash cards
* make a bingo game and calling cards
* use for spelling lists
* copy for homework

* Enlarge the pictures for work with younger students
* Put one enlarged verb picture per page. Then have the student copy the verb and write the word again. Finally, the student is to write a simple sentence.

Basic Verbs Picture Vocabulary

Go through the verb picture pages one at a time with students. See which students know the verbs. Use peer translation and mime as needed to ensure comprehension. Students should copy the verbs under their pictures as you pronounce and write them.

Page 1

cry	drink	draw	eat
grow	fall	swim	climb
paint	write	wash	ride
stand	watch	talk	sit
pick	forget	hit	play

Page 2

sleep	break	fly	fight
catch	read	jump	kick
run	open close	drive	put
cut	walk	throw	carry or bring
choose	find	look	turn

Page 3

pull	steal	fix	laugh
drop	smell	hear	give
ask	cook	dance	save
melt	dream	brush	think
sing	call	come	blow

* Use the same pictures for past tense verb vocabulary.
* Use the vocabulary for spelling lists.
* Make 2 piles of pictures – those with -ed past tense endings, and those which do not (irregular past tenses)

Past Tense Verb Pictures

Write the past tense verbs in the correct picture box.

slept	chose	stood
broke	found	watched
flew	looked	talked
fought	turned	sat
caught	cried	picked
read	drank	forgot
jumped	drew	hit
kicked	ate	played
ran	grew	pulled
opened	fell	stole
drove	swam	fixed
put	climbed	laughed
cut	painted	dropped
walked	wrote	smelled
threw	washed	heard
carried	rode	gave

 # Bingo Games

What is Bingo?

Bingo is a game that includes listening, speaking, and sometimes reading. Bingo is used to review and practice new vocabulary. Originally, Bingo was played with numbers. However, Language Bingo uses pictures, words or both. Students love Bingo because it's fun, fast paced, and they could win.

How Do You Play Language Bingo?

Bingo is played on a sheet of paper with a grid of squares. Inside each square is a picture or a new vocabulary word. Although each Bingo sheet has the same pictures, the pictures are located in different squares. Every student has one Bingo sheet and a pile of 20 or more poker chips or colored circles.

The object of the game is to be the first person to cover a line of squares with tokens when a word or clue is called. Then students must shout out, "Bingo!" to tell everyone they won. The line may be vertical or horizontal.

The "caller" is the person who has a deck of cards with all the pictures. The deck is shuffled and placed face down. The caller says the picture-word, as a card is turned up, then shows it to the players, and repeats the word.

Students listen to the word, locate it on their Bingo sheet, and place a token on top of that picture. This continues until a student shouts "Bingo".

When a student shouts "Bingo!" everybody stops until the line is checked. The student has to uncover the line of objects and say each picture to verify the win. Usually the winner gets a little prize such as a sticker, balloon or pen. Sometimes several students will call Bingo at the same time, so there could be two or three winners.

Use Bingo as a listening activity with new vocabulary. Enunciate clearly. The next time students play the same Bingo, say the word and then use it in a phrase or sentence. For example, book – my book – Where is my book?

When students know the words, they will want to become the caller. In this way, teachers can assess a student's pronunciation and speech.

Play the same BINGO several times.
Each time, students will remember more.
Each time, a new student gets to be a caller.
Each time, teachers get to assess pronunciation.
Each time, the word can be used in different ways;
in a single word, a phrase, a sentence, or a riddle.

Why Bingo?

Bingo provides for an essential review of vocabulary as students have fun listening and helping each other find the right pictures.

Bingo requires active participation as students are engaged in looking, listening and identifying the appropriate picture.

Bingo lets the teacher enunciate each individual word carefully before extending language use by putting the word in context or a riddle, which is pretty tricky, but forces the kids to speak out.

Bingo allows the teacher an opportunity to assess student spoken language and pronunciation as they repeat the words and talk amongst themselves.

Use poker chips instead of Bingo chips
because they are bigger, more colorful and are not transparent.
If you can't find inexpensive poker chips then cut out multiple
small squares of colored stock card
or find something similar in the Dollar Store.

Pair Cards or Bingo Calling Card Form

Match the Verbs

sleep

smell

bring

want

brush

- brought
- smelled
- looked
- dreamt
- slept
- brushed
- fought
- found
- blew
- wanted

dream

look

blow

find

fight

Verbs

Draw a stickman for each verb.

ate	went	saw	broke
knew	blew	grew	flew
said	brought	fought	caught
spoke	slept	heard	rode

Verbs

Draw a stickman for each verb.

came	drove	hit	told
gave	ran	drew	sold
bought	cut	found	stood
threw	thought	hid	wrote

Magazine Verb Books
Skills – speaking, listening, reading, writing, spelling, and/or past tense verbs

Collect a variety of suitable magazines that students can use to cut out pictures. Ask your librarian for old science, wildlife, sports or teen magazines. You could also send a note home to parents asking for suitable magazines. Fashion magazines do not generally depict a wide variety of verb pictures, and Newsweek magazines often show violent scenes – so you might want to exclude these kinds.

The Activity, Duration 5-6 Sessions

1. Start by showing students examples of verbs that you cut from magazines and glued onto colored construction paper. The samples should have the word printed from a computer, and then pasted under the picture.
- Samples should show pictures that are large, with a computer font and size that make the verb words **large and clear**. (size 18 or larger)
- Book a time in the school computer lab for your students to type in and print out their verb words once the cut and paste activity is completed.
- Students should work in groups of 4. This number allows English language learners to hear the ideas of others, verbalize comfortably at their level of fluency, and get help as needed. Teachers can ask group members to either work on a book of their own, or to compile verb pictures as a group, in which case there shouldn't be duplicates.

2. Students should save their pictures in their workbook or a file folder with their name, and cut pictures from a variety of magazines over 2 days.

3. Ask volunteers to show samples which clearly illustrate the large, clear, or humorous pictures before students start cutting on the second day.

4. Assign another day to paste the verb pictures on background paper.

5. Students use the computer to type, spell check and print their words.

6. Share the verb books with each other in class.

Brainstorming

Use the following pages to teach and/or review the concept of 'brainstorming'. The words 'brain' and 'storm' may also need to be translated and acted out for the first few lessons.

Each picture can be used in two different ways.
* First, to elicit a large numbers of verbs occurring in a topic
* Second, to train students to break down a large topic into sub-topics, and then to list detail words.
  See examples that follow.

How to use the picture prompts:

Enlarge a picture and have the students cut and glue it in the middle of a large sheet of easel paper. Students should work in groups of 3's to provide risk-free, supported learning.

At that point, students work with the teacher who guides the process of brainstorming.

If the activity is for paragraphing, again the teacher guides the process with the students for several lessons.

①

WINTER

throw　　　　　　　　　　slip
make　　　　　　　　　　slide
put　　　　　　　　　　　fall
play　　　　　　　　　　 roll
skate　　　　　　　　　　build
ski　　　　　　　　　　　shovel
toboggan　snoeshoe　wear

②

- When + Weather
- Special Days
- Activities Sports
- Problems

WINTER

FALL

SPRING

WINTER

SUMMER

SPORTS

IN THE PARK

AT HOME

IN THE GYM

More Verbs - Past Tense

1. The ending *-ed* can show the past tense of verbs.

   Example : play - play<u>ed</u>

   walk - _____   wait - _____
   burn - _____   fix - _____
   call - _____   push - _____

2. If a verb ends in *-e*, just add the *-d*

   Example : hate - hate<u>d</u>

   die - _____   arrive - _____
   bake - _____   like - _____
   shove - _____ hire - _____

3. With a one syllable word ending in 1 vowel and 1 consonant, you double the final consonant and add *-ed*.

   Example : drop - drop<u>ped</u>

   stop - _____   clap - _____
   tap - _____   rub - _____
   tug - _____   flip - _____

4. Many verbs are tricky. They are called irregular past tense verbs. You will have to practice and memorize them.

   Example : see - saw

   run - _____   go - _____
   say - _____   write - _____
   eat - _____   know - _____

Teacher Information for Verbs of State

In English grammar, a *stative verb* is a verb used to describe a state of being (I *am*) or situation (I *have*). It's how something **is**, **feels**, or **appears**. These verbs don't show physical action (I *run*) Stative verbs can describe a mental or emotional state of being (I *doubt*) as well as a physical state (Peter *was* here).

Verbs that express a state rather than an action usually relate to thoughts, emotions, relationships, senses, and states of being. Common examples include *be, have, like, seem, prefer, understand, belong, doubt, hate,* and *know*.

Senses and perception verbs include data coming into your five senses:

- See Hear Smell Taste See

Emotion and thought verbs include:

- Love Hate Adore Like Despise Doubt Feel Believe Forget Remember Agree
- Enjoy Need Think Recognize Prefer Understand Suspect Appear

Possession verbs include:

- Have Belong Include Own Want

Verbs that describe states of being include:

- Be/Are/Is Weigh Contain Involve Consist

Teachers ought to introduce this concept in a simple, direct way. The main idea is for students to understand that they are verbs. Students do not need to memorize the definition. Following is a student activity to identify the verb.

Underline the Verbs.   Name _____

1. I **know** the answer. You **don't**.   (don't = do not)

2. She **needs** her mother because she **feels** really sick.

3. I **want** a cookie but I **hate** that kind.

4. I **think** it**'s** Monday, but I **am** not sure.   (I am = I'm)

5. Yes, we **like** TV shows, but we **love** movies more.

6. I **think** he **lied**, and I **believe** you.

7. Please **taste** this for me. It might **be** too spicy.

8. I **smell** smoke. **Do** you?

9. He only **has** enough money for a hamburger.

10. I **understand** the question, but it **confuses** me.

11. I **hate** eggs. They **are** gross.   (They are = They're)

12. I **remember** now. I **agree** with you that the accident **was** his fault.

13. I **am** really tired. I **need** a nap.

14. Who **owns** the red car? I **do**.

15. They **weighed** me in the doctor's office. I **look** skinny, but I **am** strong.

16. He **wants** a truck not a car. I **forget** which kind.

17. This dog **belongs** to that guy. He **owns** it.

Do You Know These Past Tense Verbs?

1. I go home after school, but yesterday I _____ to the doctor.
   go _____

2. Can I come to your house? You _____ to my house yesterday.
   come _____

3. If you're lucky, you'll win the lottery. You _____ the race.
   win _____

4. Write the past tense of these verbs.

   eat _____
   make _____
   grow _____
   give _____
   know _____
   draw _____
   send _____
   fall _____
   meet _____
   find _____
   feel _____
   think _____
   bring _____
   catch _____
   drink _____

Past Tense Practice

Say these verbs.

say   said   see   saw

go   went   hear   heard

make   made   build built

Write the past tense.

see _____   make _____

go _____   say _____

build _____   hear _____

Write the correct verb.

1. My mom _____ a great dinner.

2. I _____ a wonderful movie.

3. He _____,"Thank you."

4. We _____ to the library to study.

5. Who _____ this building?

6. I _____ this song before.

Change a Word
Take turns. You can change letters, or add letters, or delete letters.

<u>s</u>end

s<u>a</u>nd

san<u>g</u>

s<u>i</u>ng

<u>br</u>ing

<u>th</u>ing

thin<u>k</u>

Verb Tense Practice

Write the missing tenses of the verbs.

PAST	PRESENT	FUTURE
cried		
	play	
		will go
	keep	
bought		
	grow	
	help	
wrote		
went		
		will clean
	bring	
		am going to run
		am going to see

The present tense is now.

The past tense is before.

The future tense is later.

Past Tense	Present Tense	Future Tense
sang	sing	will sing

Write the past and future tenses of these verbs.

Past Tense	Present Tense	Future Tense
	laugh	
	buy	
	speak	
	give	
	throw	
	write	
	tell	

Verb Tense Practice

Write the missing tenses of the verbs.

PAST	PRESENT	FUTURE
bought		
	sell	
		will tell
	get	
kept		
	leave	
	lose	
hurt		
won		
		will forget
	cost	
		am going to copy
		am going to put

NOTE – These verbs have the same past tense as their present tense (very tricky).
put   hit   cut   hurt

Verbs - Future Tense Forms

There are several ways to indicate the future tense in English.

1. "Will" plus verb – indicates a promise or strong determination.
   For example - I **will pass** the test.
                 He **will buy** a car.
                 I **won't cut** my hair.   I **will not** = I **won't**

2. "Is/am/are going to" plus verb – shows an intention or plan.
   For example - She **is going to visit** the doctor after school.
                 I **am going to watch** T.V. now.
                 They **are going to play** soccer.

3. "Might" plus verb – means a future possibility
   For example – I **might go** to Canada.
                 We **might play** basketball tonight.
                 She **might help** you.

4. "Would" or "could" plus verb – shows a conditional action
   For example – I **would go** with you if I have enough time.
                 They **would buy** a house if they won a lottery.
                 He **could watch** T.V. if he finishes homework.
                 It **could rain** this afternoon.

5. "Might be" or "could be" – a present or future possibility
   For example – This **might be** a mistake.
                 They **might be** lost.
                 He **might be** in love with you.
                 It **could be** a scary movie.

Future Tense Forms

1. **WILL**

    shows a strong determination or a promise

    i.e.,   *He will succeed!*
    I will pay my bills!

2. **IS/AM GOING TO**

    shows an intention or a plan

    i.e.,   *She is going shopping this afternoon.*
    We're going to a movie tonight.

3. **MIGHT/WOULD/COULD**

    shows a possibility in the future, and future conditional

    i.e.,   *I might go to Disney world.*
    He would come with us tomorrow, but he has to work.
    My brother could help you on Saturday, if you need him.

Activities to teach the future tense forms

- *Make plans for the weekend. Use all 3 forms.*

- *Make a list of things you promise to do for your mother on Mother's Day/Father's Day.*

- *Make New Years Resolution promises.*

- *Wow! You won $5 million in the lottery. Write three paragraphs telling what you will do with all that money. Use all the different future forms.*

Teaching Modals (helping verbs)

- *Cut out a large picture and cover all but one part. Students compose a sentence pattern about what your picture is, i.e.,* **It might/could be a...**

- *Draw a nonsensical squiggle on a sheet of paper. Students complete a drawing using that same line and then compose a sentence as follows:* **It might / could be a...**

Future Tense Verbs

I will = a promise

I'm going to = a plan

I might = a possibility

1. What have you promised your mom?

I will _____

I will _____

I will _____

2. What are you doing this weekend?

I'm going to/ I'm gunna _____

I'm going to _____

I'm going to _____

3. What are you going to do when you are an adult?

I might _____

I might _____

I might _____

Will Not = Won't

Change the verb 'will not' to won't in these sentences.

1. He will not help me.
   He _____ help me.

2. I will not finish this much pizza.
   I _____ finish this much pizza.

3. She will not have enough money to go out.
   She _____ have enough money to go out.

4. There will not be a test tomorrow.
   There _____ be a test tomorrow.

5. He will not go to horror movies.
   He _____ go to horror movies.

6. My mom will not let me go with you.
   My mom _____ let me go with you.

7. The TV will not work.
   The TV _____ work.

8. She will not be able to come to my birthday party.
   She _____ be able to come to my birthday party.

Would
Conditional

1. If I had a million dollars, I would _____

2. If my mom was sick. she would _____

3. If we had no fire alarm, we _____

4. If I were old enough, I would _____

5. If a bear came, I would _____

I would = I'd

he would = he'd

They would = They'd

1. If I were lost, _____

2. They'd get in trouble if they _____

3. If we went out at night, _____

4. If I were a genius, _____

5. If he had studied, he'd have _____

Past Tense Practice

Say these verbs.

give	gave		run	ran
drink	drank		sing	sang
come	came		swim	swam

Write the past tense.

swim _____   drink _____

run _____   give _____

drink _____   sing _____

Write the correct verb.

1. My mom _____ to see my teacher.

2. I _____ in the pool in my building.

3. We _____ her a birthday present.

4. They _____ in the choir.

5. I was so thirsty I _____ all the coke.

6. He was late so he _____ to school.

Past Tense Patterns

A) Read these rows of verbs. Translate any you don't know.
B) What's the same about the verbs in each row?
C) Underline the **pattern**.

1. bought   fought   brought   thought   caught   taught
2. blew   knew   grew   drew   flew   threw
3. spoke   broke
4. wore   tore

- Now write the past tense of each verb.

fight _____   buy _____   think _____
bring _____   catch _____   teach _____
know _____   grow _____   fly _____
blow _____   draw _____   throw _____
speak _____   break _____
tear _____   wear _____

- Write your own ideas with the past tense verbs.

_____
_____
_____
_____
_____
_____

Past Tense Practice

Say these verbs.

write	wrote	drive	drove
speak	spoke	ride	rode
break	broke	wake	woke

Write the past tense.

drive _____   break _____

write _____   ride _____

speak _____   wake _____

Write the correct verb.

1. My parents _____ me to school.

2. I _____ up at 8 o'clock.

3. She _____ the best story.

4. I'm sorry. I _____ your pen.

5. I couldn't hear her. She _____ so softly.

Past Tense Practice

Say these verbs.

draw	drew	grow	grew
know	knew	blow	blew
throw	threw	fly	flew

Write the past tense.

blow _____   grow _____

know _____   fly _____

throw _____   draw _____

Write the correct verb.

1. My mother's flowers _____.

2. I _____ the answer.

3. She _____ the baseball so far.

4. The wind _____ my hat off.

5. My bird _____ away.

6. He _____ a beautiful picture.

Past Tense Practice

Say these verbs.

cost	cost	leave	left
lose	lost	tell	told
forget	forgot	sell	sold

Write the past tense.

tell _____   sell _____

forget _____   cost _____

leave _____   lose _____

Write the correct past tense verb.

1. I'm going to get in trouble. I _____ my backpack.

2. His parents _____ to go to Hawaii.

3. I asked,"How much?" She said it _____ $400.

4. I _____ everybody about my accident.

5. We _____ our house, yesterday.

6. Oh no! I _____ to bring my note back to school.

Past Tense Practice

Say these verbs.

buy	bought	think	thought
bring	brought	fight	fought
catch	caught	teach	taught

Write the past tense.

teach _____   catch _____

buy _____   bring _____

think _____   fight _____

Write the correct verb.

1. My mom _____ me how to cook.

2. She _____ a new sweater.

3. He _____ money to buy pizza.

4. I _____ today was Friday.

5. I _____ a big fish.

6. Those guys _____ each other.

Past Tense Practice

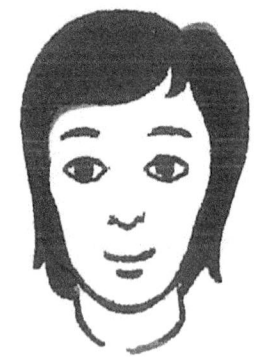

Say these verbs.

feel	felt	meet	met
spend	spent	keep	kept
lend	lent	dream	dreamt

Write the past tense.

keep _____   feel _____

meet _____   spend _____

lend _____   dream _____

Write the correct past tense verb.

1. Last night, I _____ about a monster.

2. My friend _____ me enough money for the bus.

3. When I _____ sick, my mom said, "Stay home."

4. I _____ the new gym teacher today.

5. He _____ all his money on a new bike.

6. My mom _____ her money in the bank.

have to

In speech 'have to' is usually pronounced – hafta.

Definition; must, need to, required to

1. I have to go to school.
2. I have to study.
3. You have to hit the ball.
4. We have to go to the gym now.
5. They have to practise soccer skills.
6. <u>He has</u> to type his work on the computer.
7. <u>She has</u> to work with a partner.

Write sentences.

1. _____
2. _____
3. _____
4. _____

Past Tense Practice

- Finish
    1. I lost _____
    2. We forgot _____
    3. He hid _____
    4. My sister sent _____
    5. She got _____
    6. She shook _____
    7. My mother made _____
    8. I kept _____
    9. I held _____
    10. I used _____
    11. Everyone put _____
    12. I had _____
    13. Last week, I lost _____
    14. My friend tore _____
    15. They got _____
    16. The father fed _____
    17. Yesterday, I spent _____
    18. She wore _____
    19. It was expensive. It cost _____
    20. Last night, I dreamt _____

- Write the past tenses.

come	_____	bend	_____
make	_____	send	_____
know	_____	lend	_____
sing	_____	do	_____
use	_____	cut	_____
hit	_____	cost	_____

Past Tense Practice

- Finish
    1. I kept _____
    2. He studied _____
    3. He drank _____
    4. The strong man bent _____
    5. We ran into _____
    6. She took _____
    7. My mother made _____
    8. I felt _____
    9. We found _____
    10. I heard _____
    11. No one understood _____
    12. I thought _____
    13. This morning, I woke _____
    14. My teacher taught _____
    15. They fought _____
    16. The seagulls flew _____
    17. Yesterday, I bought _____
    18. At the ball game I caught _____
    19. My brother forgot _____
    20. I spent _____

- Make the past tenses.

    blow - _____   buy - _____
    know - _____   fight - _____
    grow - _____   bring - _____
    draw - _____   think - _____
    fly - _____   teach - _____
    throw - _____   catch - _____

Past Tense Practice

- **Finish**
    1. I sat _____
    2. We gave _____
    3. He told _____
    4. The ice _____ on the lake.
    5. We hid from _____
    6. I shook _____
    7. My mother took _____
    8. I sold _____
    9. I thought _____
    10. I began _____
    11. No one said _____
    12. They rode _____
    13. She knew _____
    14. My friend fell _____
    15. I kept _____
    16. The baby felt _____
    17. Last night, I held _____
    18. They _____ down deep to build a tunnel.
    19. Wow! You grew _____
    20. I hate that guy. He hit_____

- **Make the past tenses.**

    sit - _____   hold - _____
    hit - _____   swim - _____
    say - _____   send - _____
    sell - _____   take - _____
    put - _____   feel - _____
    eat - _____   bite - _____

Past Tense Practice

1. He _____ all his money. (lose)
2. She _____ the vegetables for dinner. (cut)
3. We _____ to the movies. (go)
4. I _____ my homework this morning. (do)
5. That little kid _____ my friend. (hit)
6. I _____ sorry. (is)
7. They _____ a new library. (build)
8. You _____ me, didn't you? (see)
9. I _____ about you last night. (dream)
10. He _____ the wrong answer. (choose)
11. The dog _____ the stranger. (bite)
12. She _____ her hair and it looks great. (cut)
13. I _____ a horse before. (ride)
14. The teacher _____ to study. (say)
15. The sun _____ at 5:30 this morning. (rise)
16. The telephone _____ but I didn't hear it. (ring)
17. We _____ the answers on a computer. (write)
18. His brother _____ himself on the rocks. (hurt)

Past Tense Practice

Change the present tense verb to the past and finish each sentence.

1. I _____ my arm in the gym. (break)

2. She _____ a new coat for winter. (buy)

3. We _____ to this city last year. (come)

4. My teacher _____ 2 coffees this morning. (drink)

5. That lucky kid _____ $ 50. (find)

6. I'm sorry. I _____ your name. (forget)

7. The boss just _____ us more work to do. (give)

8. You _____ me, didn't you? (hear)

9. I _____ I _____ you. (think) (know)

10. Too bad! He _____ the money. (lose)

11. We _____ the new student yesterday. (meet)

12. You _____ your books over there last night. (put)

13. I _____ the subway to go downtown. (ride)

14. The old lady _____ who _____ it. (see) (do)

15. The principal _____ to us. (speak)

16. Our teacher _____ a bad cold. (catch)

17. We _____ the answers on a computer. (write)

18. I _____ even thought I _____ sick. (come) (feel)

19. She _____ a Chinese dictionary. (bring)

20. They _____ not ready, so we _____. (are) (leave)

21. On the weekend, we _____ to a movie. (go)

22. The little girl _____ her knee. (cut)

23. He _____ chicken-pox last summer. (have)

24. I'm glad I _____ my sweater today. It's cold out! (wear)

25. We _____ in the pool at the community center. (swim)

26. John _____ in late so he _____ in trouble. (sleep) (get)

27. I _____ so hungry that I _____ too much. (am) (eat)

28. The news _____ he _____ off a cliff. (say) (fall)

29. My dog _____ a hole and _____ his bone. (dig) (bury)

30. We _____ for 4 hours during the concert. (stand)

Past Tense Practice

Do you remember the past tense of these verbs?

write _____   fight _____

have _____   grow _____

forget _____   eat _____

catch _____   run _____

give _____   make _____

sleep _____   find _____

fall _____   see _____

read _____   put _____

break _____   sell _____

freeze _____   go _____

come _____   sing _____

sit _____   do _____

know _____   steal _____

take _____   drive _____

get _____   throw _____

hear _____   feel _____

 Hooray! You're done.

Helping Verbs

Examples - do, did, does, may might, should, would, could, was, were, can, have, has, had, must, ought, shall, used to

Circle the helping verbs in these sentences.

1. He ought to study before 10 o'clock, or he may fall asleep.
2. I shall give more money to poor people.
3. He has to stop his homework now.
4. She ought to win first prize for her story.
5. I can do the homework later tonight.
6. The dog has chewed all my shoes.
7. You should stretch first or you could get sore muscles.
8. Did you get the marks back from your test?
9. He used to ski.
10. You did not try hard enough.
11. I could swim across that lake.
12. Could I borrow some money?
13. It might rain tomorrow. I might stay home.
14. Don't count on me for a ride. I might be too busy.
15. Shall I help you with those bags?
16. My friend said that he would help me.
17. There used to be an office over there.
18. Everybody must obey the law.

Infinitives

Infinitives are any verb with a 'TO' in front.
Infinitives are NOT the main verb.
Example – to run, to play, to catch, to fly

- Write an Infinitive verb in these sentences.

1. I like _____ baseball.

2. He wants _____ with you.

3. I forget _____ the milk.

4. We would like _____ the museum.

5. I decided not _____ to school today.

- Now, finish these sentences using an Infinitive.

1. I am waiting _____

2. John tried _____

3. They intended _____

4. Mary hoped _____

5. The teacher ordered her _____

6. My mom allowed me _____

7. I'd love _____

8. My boss advised me _____

9. His father asked him _____

10. I promise _____

Give Suggestions or Advice

1. Listen and pronounce this vocabulary.

should	could have
shouldn't	might have
ought to	had better
have to	must
have got to	It's necessary
recommend	suggest that

2. Read these examples about suggestions and advice.

   a) You <u>should</u> go to the dentist.
   b) You <u>should not</u> eat ice when you have a sore tooth.
   c) You <u>could have</u> studied instead of watching TV.
   d) She <u>ought to</u> practice more if she really wants to win.
   e) You <u>have got to</u> finish this before you go to sleep.
   f) We <u>have to</u> go to sleep now.
   g) I <u>recommend</u> that you get more exercise.
   h) You <u>might have</u> asked for help with the math homework.
   i) She <u>must</u> hurry up or she'll miss her bus.
   j) He <u>suggested that</u> I stop all my bad habits.
   k) The doctor said <u>it is necessary</u> to get this operation.

3. Write your own sentences to give advice.

4. Which words are the most formal?

5. Which words do you use as contractions when you speak? for example – it's

Teachers,

Introduce new lessons with a 'talking session' that uses the verb concept/tense in normal circumstances. Then guide students as they work with the practise sheet. This develops real communicative speech with students since they experience the verb form in natural conversation. Elementary grade students do not need to memorize the terms.

Examples:

1. Gerunds - talk about what students like to do, reading, swimming, and/or what jobs they do at home, vacuuming, washing, cooking. With each idea that students have, provide an answer with the gerund form, such as," Yes, swimming is great exercise. Cooking is work but baking is fun." Students will hear gerunds being used in a real conversation, and then they will better understand the activity sheet.

2. Perfect Tenses - Try a student survey with short questions using, Have you ever been bullied? Have you seen a rainbow? Have you ridden a horse/camel? Have you flown in a plane? Have you ever broken a bone? Has your family ever been robbed? Etc. You could also start a lesson with one of the above questions and elicit a general response so students can hear lots of answers and perhaps offer longer discourse.

Gerunds

A Gerund is a noun-verb with -ing.

Example – reading, sleeping, helping, skiing

- Finish these sentences with an -ing verb.

1. I like _____ .

2. My mother began _____ the cookbook.

3. He started _____ for his test last night.

4. We have finished _____ .

5. Don't keep _____ that.

6. My sister enjoys _____ the piano.

7. I don't like _____ those vegetables.

8. I hate _____ .

9. Stop _____ so much.

10. Do you remember _____ ?

* * * * * * * * * * * * * * * *

- Finish these sentences.

1. Playing tennis is _____

2. Reading is _____

3. Speaking English is _____

4. Spelling is _____

5. Dancing is _____

6. Singing is _____

Adverbs

What is an adverb?

> An Adverb describes a verb; they tell 'how'.
>
> Example 1, Joe <u>ran</u>. Joe ran <u>fast</u>. Joe ran <u>silently</u>.
>   verb   verb adverb   verb adverb
>
> Example 2, I whispered quietly, slowly, softly, and sweetly.

> An Adverb also tells 'when'.
>
> Example 1, Joe <u>slept</u>. Joe slept <u>late</u>. Joe <u>always</u> slept.
>   verb   verb adverb   adverb verb
>
> Example 2, I whispered quietly, slowly, softly, and sweetly.

> Words with -ly are adverbs. Read these adverbs.
>
> | slowly | neatly | cleverly | softly |
> |---|---|---|---|
> | angrily | quickly | brightly | easily |
> | happily | loudly | thoughtfully | silently |

Write 10 sentences with an adverb.

Adverbs

1. Some adverbs tell how something happens.
Many adverbs end in –ly.
slowly – softly – quickly – carefully – nervously – sweetly – cleverly
happily – comfortably - dangerously – carefully – rapidly - neatly

2. Choose an adverb and fill in the blanks.

The sun shone _____. (brightly, gloriously)

She finished the test _____. (quickly, carefully)

Her baby cries _____. (loudly, constantly)

He always does his work _____. (carefully, cautiously)

My friend whispered _____to me. (quietly, softly)

He _____ figured it out. (cleverly, easily)

The wind blew_____. (gently, softly)

He rode _____. (dangerously, carefully)

3. Make 4 of your own sentences using adverbs.

_____

_____

_____

_____

Adverbs Help Verbs

Adverbs tell **how** something happens or **when**.

Here are some examples of adverbs that tell 'how'.
    softly   quickly   sadly   easily

He speaks (how) - softly.
I ran (how) - quickly.
She answered the questions (how) - easily.
The child cried (how) - sadly.

Here are some examples of adverbs that tell 'when'.
    early now soon later never always often

I arrived (when) - early.
She'll visit you (when) - soon.
The show is on (when) - later.
He is here (when) - now.

Finish these sentences with an adverb.

1. The moon shines _____. (how)

2. I feel _____ by myself. (how)

3. He whispered _____ to me. (how)

4. The bus will come _____. (when)

5. She's going _____. (when)

6. I _____ go on the Internet. (when)

Adverbs

Some adverbs tell when or how often something happens.
They are called adverbs of frequency.

---

1. Read these adverbs.

		2. Read these sentences
always	never	a) He's always late.
usually	hardly ever	b) I hardly ever eat pizza.
sometimes	seldom	c) Sometimes, I daydream.
often	rarely	d) I rarely save money.
probably	already	e) She's probably sick.
frequently	occasionally	f) I skate occasionally.

---

3. Fill in the blanks with your choice of an adverb of frequency.

My mom _____ goes shopping. (usually, often, always)

I _____ lose my wallet. (seldom, rarely, never)

We _____ have homework. (frequently, usually, often)

You _____ make a mistake. (occasionally, rarely, seldom)

You're _____ right. (never, always, hardly ever)

Babies _____ have soft skin. (usually, always, often)

He _____ goes to a movie. (seldom, occasionally, never)

We _____ does homework. (often, always, usually)

Two Word Verbs

Listen to your teacher pronounce and explain meanings. Listen to the sample sentences. Write a sentence for each two word verb.

1. look up

2. stand up

3. get up

4. go up

5. tie up

6. put the  up

7. clean up

8. pick up

9. make up

10. wake up

Two Word Verb Expressions
Comprehension of Idiomatic Two-Word Verbs

Listen - Listen to the teacher read and explain the 2-word verbs below.
Speak - Say other sentences using the same verb.
Write - Write a sentence of your own.

act up - That little kid acts up all the time.
_____

cover up - The boss has to cover up his theft from the company.
_____

bring up - The doctor said that I would probably bring up.
_____

bring up - I want to bring up that idea during our discussion?
_____

dream up - How did she dream up that idea?
_____

use up - If you use up all the ketchup, let me know.
_____

give up - Daniel had to give up music.
_____

fix up - Fix up this mess right now.
_____

fix up - She should fix up her work.
_____

take up - My brother is going to take up golf this summer.
_____

Two Word Verbs

Read these verbs

put on	take off	turn on	turn off
get on	get off	get out	
blow up	blow out		
look at	look after	look up	look over
wake up	clean up	turn up	
figure out	write down	hand in	

Read these sentences.

1. It's cold out. Put on your coat.
2. Take off your coat.
3. Please turn on the lights.
4. Could you turn off the lights, please?
5. Get on the bus. Get off the subway.
6. Get out of here. Get out your dictionary.
7. Blow up the balloons. Blow out the candles.
8. Look at this. Look after the baby.
9. Look up the word in your dictionary.
10. The teacher said to look over the spelling words.
11. I can't figure out the answer. Can you?
12. Write down these words. Hand in your test.
13. Wake up now. You have to clean up your room.
14. Please, turn up the T.V. I can't hear it.

More Two-Word Verbs

make up = 1. imagine (make up a story)
       = 2. cosmetics (put on my makeup)

watch out = 1. be careful (watch out for danger)
        = 2. look & see (Watch out for cars.)

find out = get the answer (Find out where he lives.)

blast off = leave fast (10-9-8-7-6-5-4-3-2-1, blast off)

take off = 1. go, leave (We have to take off now.)
       = 2. remove (Please, take off your shoes.)

grow up = 1. become older (When I grow up, I'll be rich.)
       = 2. get bigger (That flower will grow up high.)

hang up = 1. stop the phone call (Hang up the phone now)
       = 2. put something up (Please hang up your coat.)
                              (Help hang up the picture.)

forget about it = 1. don't worry (Forget about the dog.)
              2. a thank you is not needed

get away = 1. leave (Get away from there.)
        = 2. a vacation (He needs to get away and relax.)

Two Word Verbs

1. Read these two-word verbs.
2. Listen to examples. Then write the meanings.
3. Write a sentence for the verbs.

cross out =
run out of =
run out for =
do over =
get through =
get back from =
turn to =
fill in =
fill out =
give up =
leave out =
tear up =
tear off =
drop in =
drop out =
fool around =

Please Look Out!

A) What do these verbs mean? Talk about it with a partner.
   Talk about it with the teacher, and write a sentence as an example.

1. look after _____

2. look at _____

3. look out _____

4. look out for _____

5. look up _____

6. look into _____

7. look down on _____

8. look over _____

B) Match the correct verb above to the meaning below.

1. review the information _____

2. be careful _____

3. find in the dictionary _____

4. watch the baby _____

5. see out the window _____

6. investigate _____

Preposition Meanings

Read these prepositions and the meanings

1. Get out. = Leave

2. Let's get out of here. = Go

3. Get out your math book. = Put your math book on the desk.

4. Take out your math book. = Put your math book on your desk.

5. Take out the garbage. = Bring the garbage outside.

6. Look out! = Danger. Be careful.

7. Watch out! = Danger possible. Be careful.

8. Find out. = Learn the answer.

9. Pick out what you want. = Choose something you want.

10. The teacher ran out of paper. = no more paper

Two Word Verb Expressions
Comprehension of Idiomatic Two-Word Verbs

Listen – Listen to the teacher read and explain the examples below.
Speak – Give examples of other sentences using the same verb.
Write – Write a sentence of your own.

grow up – He grew up with five sisters.
_____

hang up – It's rude to hang up on somebody.
_____

lighten up – He has to lighten up, or he'll drive us crazy.
_____

sign up – If you want to play baseball, you have to sign up today.
_____

keep up – They can't keep up with the work.
_____

make up – She don't know how to make up with her boyfriend.
_____

make up – You have to make-up for the work you missed.
_____

think up – We need to think up an excuse for skipping class.
_____

straighten up – She had better straighten up her room.
_____

stay up – Andy stayed up all night watching T.V.
_____

Two Word Verb Expressions
Comprehension of Idiomatic Two-Word Verbs

Listen – Listen to the teacher read and explain the 2-word verbs below.
Speak – Say examples of sentences using the same verb.
Write - Write a sentence of your own.

grow up – He grew up with five sisters.
_____

hang up – It's rude to hang up on somebody.
_____

lighten up – He has to lighten up, or he'll drive us crazy.
_____

sign up – If you want to play baseball, you have to sign up today.
_____

keep up – She can't keep up with the work. She needs help.
_____

make up – She doesn't want to make up with her boyfriend.
_____

make up – You have to make-up for the work you missed.
_____

think up – We need to think up an excuse for skipping class.
_____

straighten up – She had better straighten up her room.
_____

stay up – Andy stayed up all night watching T.V.
_____

Two Word Verb Expressions
Comprehension of Idiomatic Two-Word Verbs

Listen – Listen to the teacher read and explain the 2-word verbs below.
Speak – Give examples of other sentences using the same verb.
Write – Write a sentence of your own.

lay off – He kept bugging his little brother so I told him to lay off.
_____

lay off – The company has to lay off sixteen people.
_____

show off – He always shows off. He's a show off.
_____

let off – The judge let off the thief with a warning this time.
_____

set off – Somebody set off the fire alarm.
_____

made off with – The thief made off with our TV, DVD player and computer.
_____

take off – Take off out of here before they come back.
_____

sign off – Okay everybody, sign off your computer and go.
_____

get off – I have to get off the subway at the next station.
_____

cut off – My parents cut me off from any T.V. when I failed the test.
_____

Perfect Tenses

Perfect tenses always use have, has or had.

Language Learners usually have difficulty with the perfect tenses, and teachers likely will not observe language learners using them very often in either oral presentations or written assignments. An easy definition would be the one above. For more mature learners, tell them that perfect tenses always relate to time.

    i.e., I *have been* sick for a week. He *has never had* an accident.

Present and past perfect tenses could be presented without naming the skill, i.e., draw students' attention to the use of perfect tenses in a text. Also, students could be assigned to create surveys that start with "Have you ever"_____ which forces the use of the perfect tense.

- for the Perfect Continuous Tense

    (drive   has been driving)

- for the Past Perfect Continuous Tense

    (drive   had been driving)

- for the Present Perfect Tense

    (drive   has driven)

- for the Past Perfect Tense

    (drive   had driven)

Perfect is a Verb Tense

Read these verbs.

have gone   have broken   have eaten
has drawn   has bitten   have forgotten

"Have" or "has" with a verb is called
the perfect tense.

Underline the perfect tenses in these sentences.

1. I <u>have been</u> to China.

2. We <u>have bought</u> a new car.

3. She <u>has drawn</u> the best picture in the world.

4. They <u>have been</u> on vacation for 3 weeks.

5. I <u>have kept</u> every doll I ever got.

6. <u>He's wanted</u> that toy for so long. (He's = He has)

7. <u>She's failed</u> every test. Yikes! (She's = She has)

8. <u>I've gotten</u> a perfect mark on every spelling test.

9. <u>We've been</u> really busy. (We've = We have)

10. <u>They've won</u> five million dollars.

11. <u>I've tried</u> to do my best.

12. It <u>has been</u> difficult to learn English verbs.

Be Perfect

Write a sentence for these verbs.

1. have eaten
   _____

2. has forgotten
   _____

3. has frozen
   _____

4. have gone
   _____

5. have finished
   _____

6. has kept
   _____

7. has bitten
   _____

8. have written
   _____

9. have taken
   _____

10. have heard
    _____

You <u>have done</u> a great job. Keep going.

Practice Makes Perfect

Make a sentence with these perfect tense verbs.

have slept - _____

has shaken - _____

have left - _____

have known - _____

have kept - _____

has made - _____

have hurt - _____

has risen - _____

have had - _____

have caught - _____

have brought - _____

has broken - _____

has begun - _____

has done - _____

The Past is Perfect

Use "had" and the past participle of the verb in these sentences.

> For example : drive – had driven
>
> sleep – had slept

- 1. Tony and John _____ to go on a bike trip last week,
     (decide)
  but John _____ over a bump and _____ his back tire.
              (ride)   (broke)
  He _____ all about it when they talked about the trip.
       (forget)
  So, they had to change their plans.

- 2. Teresa _____ money for her birthday. She _____
              (get)   (think)
  about what she wanted and decided that she _____ enough
                                                  (buy)
  clothes, so she went to buy a CD player, instead.

- 3. Harry _____ a brand new car. He _____ on a test
             (purchase)   (go)
  drive and everything _____ O.K. but as soon as he took
                            (seem)
  the car home, it stopped. Poor Harry _____ a lemon.
                                              (buy)

- 4. Maria _____ too much again. She _____ extra
              (eat)   (take)
  turkey and gravy and two pieces of dessert. She _____
                                                       (try)
  to diet before but _____ when she hadn't lost weight.
                        (give up)

- 5. Ever since he _____ about the math test, Peter
                      (find out)
  _____ very hard. He _____ the last
       (study)   (fail)
  test and knew he had to improve his marks this time.

Have a Perfect Tense

Read a sentence. Write a sentence.

1. He <u>has chosen</u> to play the guitar. What <u>have you chosen</u>?
   _____

2. What <u>have you drawn</u>?
   _____

3. She <u>has dreamt</u> about winning the lottery for years.
   _____

4. We <u>have dug</u> a cave into the hillside. <u>I've dug</u> out a diamond.
   _____

5. His tire <u>has blown</u> so it's flat as a pancake now.
   _____

6. They <u>have gone</u> to the store. <u>They've gone</u> crazy.
   _____

7. That dog <u>has bitten</u> me twice.
   _____

8. She <u>has broken</u> my heart, and I <u>have broken</u> my glasses.
   _____

9. Who <u>has fed</u> the dog? Okay, who <u>hasn't fed</u> the dog?
   _____

10. You have grown so big! Yeah, and I've grown rich too.
_____

11. The thief has hidden in the park. He's hidden the money too.
_____

12. Mom has forgotten all about my birthday. Whaaaa! Boo hoo!
_____

13. The water has frozen so we can skate now.
_____

14. That guy has gotten into trouble before.
_____

15. She has flown a helicopter before. I've flown a paper airplane.
_____

16. The doctor has done ten surgeries today.
_____

17. I have heard that joke before.
_____

18. My grandfather has ridden an elephant. I've ridden a camel.
_____

Verbs as Cognitive Processes

In junior grades, learning becomes more challenging for students in terms of cognitive processing. This expectation is reflected in the use of verbs that require specific thinking skills.

compare
summarize
identify
discuss
predict
infer
adapt
describe
prioritize
analyze
decide
provide arguments for/against

Verb Comprehension, Cognition and Equity

There is a huge difference in the kinds of questions we ask students after the primary grades. By the time students reach grade 5, teacher expectations of student growth in maturation, logical thinking and cognitive abilities have changed and as a result the language used to elicit knowledge becomes more abstract and complex.

When teachers work on new curriculum topics, the 'what to do' or verb vocabulary could pose a major stumbling block for language learners in text questions, assignments, group talk, and tests.
The following 'what to do' verbs were taken from a grade 5 reader. Which verbs do you think your ELLs could read and pronounce correctly? Which verbs would your ELLs understand? What could you say to explain the meanings?

include	examine
apply	identify
infer	think critically
skim	predict
track	gather
jot down	state
assess	support
figure out	define
demonstrate	contrast
respond to	provide

Past Tense Practice

Say these verbs.

explain	explained	describe	described
list	listed	define	defined
discuss	discussed	identify	identified

Translate these verbs.

define _____   identify _____

list _____   explain _____

discuss _____   describe _____

Write the correct past tense verb.

1. We _____ everything we needed for the trip.

2. A dictionary _____ the word for me.

3. I _____ why I was late for class.

4. Everybody _____ the ideas in the story.

5. She _____ what the character looked like.

6. We _____ the bad guy in the story.

Summarize

Word: summarize (verb)
       summary (noun)

Definition:
to tell the main idea about what happened in a book, or a movie, or the news; to tell the important events

Example:
What was it about? Summarize it for me.

Important Vocabulary

main characters	sequence of events	genre
author	co-author	conclusion
setting	chapter	illustrator

define
definition

Define: give the exact meaning

Define the word 'easy'.
What is the definition of 'easy?

Word – easy
Definition – not difficult
Example – This work is easy.

Verbs into Nouns

1. Listen to the pronunciation of each verb and noun. Repeat each noun.
2. Mark the 'stress' syllable with the teacher's help.

1. decide   decision

2. compare   comparison

3. discuss   discussion

4. think   thought

5. prove   proof

6. summarize   summary

7. respond   response

8. achieve   achievement

9. argue   argument

10. state   statement

Verbs into Nouns

1. Listen to the pronunciation of each noun. Repeat each noun aloud.
2. Mark the 'stress' syllable along with the teacher. Repeat the noun.
3. In groups of 3, take turns pronouncing the nouns.

explain	explanátion
identify	identification
illustrate	illustration
organize	organization
investigate	investigation
educate	education
observe	observation
indicate	indication
create	creation
pronounce	pronunciation
interpret	interpretation
categorize	categorization
recognize	recognition
describe	description
predict	prediction

Compare (v)

Comparison (n)

Compare means to tell what is the same and what is different about 2 things.

Vocabulary Examples

. . . but . . .

We both are . . .

. . . is the same as . . .

. . . is different from . . .

However, . . .

Compare Summer Words

hotel and a motel

a snorkel and SCUBA

a lake and a river

a beach and a pool

a tent and a trailer

a park and a beach

a suntan and a sunburn

a holiday and a camp

contrast

Definition

to tell the differences between 2 things

Contrast these
WalMart – School

Polar bear – Panda bear

| but   however   although   is – isn't |

Examine

Definition:

to look at carefully and to find facts, details or reasons

- examine a crime scene
- examine the reasons for peace

Category (n)

Categorize (v)

A category is a group of things.

To categorize something is to:

- put the same things together,

- put different things in groups,

- to sort things into kinds/types

Talk Activity

Categorize styles of music.

Category

Categorize means to put things in groups, to sort things, to put things together that go together.

Here are some categories of			

wheels   music   places
water   people   plants
homes   vehicles   sports

Prioritize

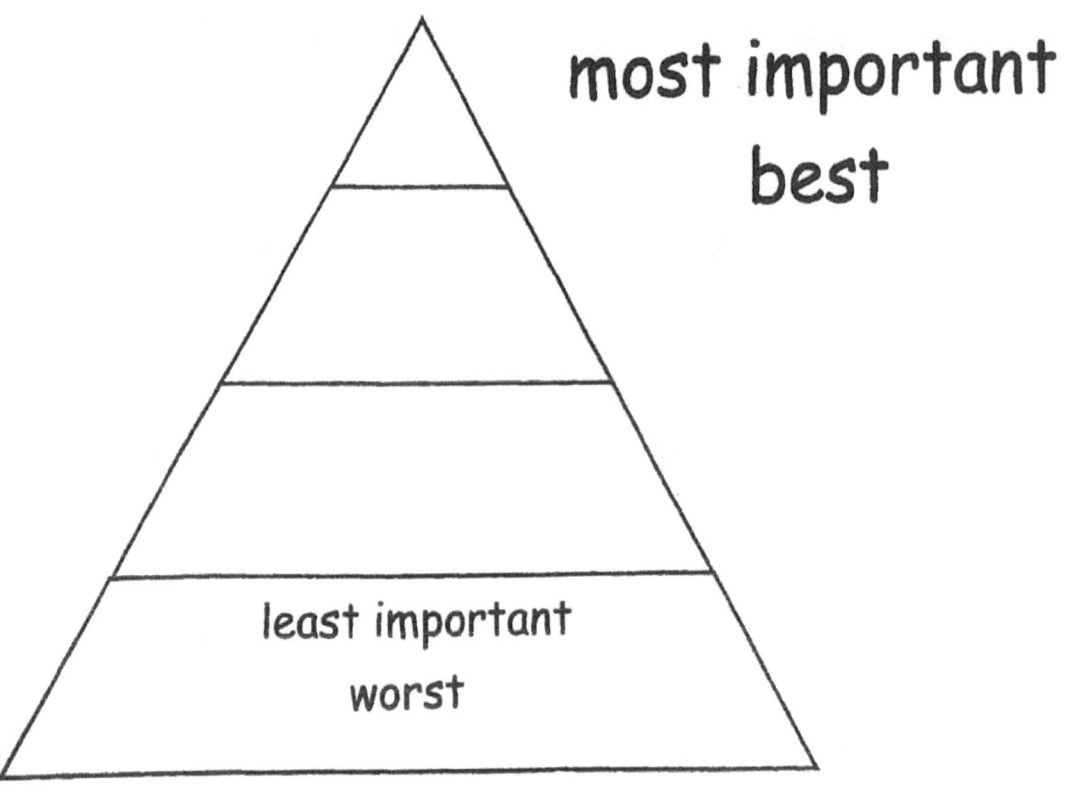

Definition:
Prioritize means to decide on the importance of things.

pri . or . i . tize

Predict

Definition:
- to say what is going to happen in the future
- to tell before it happens

Prediction

1. Predict the weather
2. Predict new inventions in medicine, space, environment

infer
inference

Definition:

To think about what happens, or what the result(s) might be. Your inferences must have good reasons, or show good judgement.

What do you infer from this sentence?
What inferences can you make?

    1. Mary is a refugee.

Analyze

Definition:

- to examine in great detail so you understand it
- to think carefully about . . .

1. Analyze the results of . . .
2. Analyze the research in . . .
3. Analyze his reasons for . . .

Verbs can tell us about moods or feelings.

Translate the verbs below. Say the words.
Share examples of these 'voice' verbs in sentences. Then write one.

1. whisper _____

2. tease _____

3. agreed _____

4. confessed _____

5. advised _____

6. sobbed _____

7. argued _____

8. admitted _____

9. quoted _____

10. groaned _____

Verb Spelling

*** Repeat these verbs after your teacher ***

agree	admit	advise	argue
explain	groan	mumble	tease
sob	describe	whisper	confess
moan	warn	yell	exclaim

1. Translate new words.
2. Discuss the meanings and say a sentence for each verb.
3. Add the past tense forms to each verb above.
4. Write the words in your workbook.
5. Make a sentence for each spelling verb.
6. Add quotation marks and correct punctuation.
7. Share examples of your work in class.
8. Pronounce each word to a partner.
9. In class, listen to the teacher's example showing how to say the words in a sentence. (intonation)
10. Share your sentences in a similar manner. (same way)

Verbs can tell us about moods or feelings.

Translate 'mood' and the verbs below. Say the words.
Share examples of these 'voice' verbs in sentences. Then write one.

1. screamed _____

2. gasped _____

3. grumbled _____

4. mumbled _____

5. pleaded _____

6. sobbed _____

7. argued _____

8. whimpered _____

9. warn _____

10. screamed _____

What Did You Say?

by _____

There are many different ways to express how someone speaks. Read the following list silently first. Then, listen as someone pronounces the words. Next, listen to the intonation when these words are put in a sentence. Finally, translate new words you don't know yet.

1. Write a sentence with each word to show meaning.

2. In groups, create a skit

a) announced _____

b) mumbled _____

c) yelled _____

d) screamed _____

e) whispered _____

f) pleaded _____

g) suggested _____

h) argued _____

i) sputtered _____

j) grumbled _____

k) exclaimed _____

l) warned _____

m) hissed _____

n) declared _____

o) complained _____

Culture

Definition:

a) A group of people with a similar way of life; with shared religion and beliefs about what is correct and acceptable in people's behaviors, the roles of women and men, in art and entertainment

b) the beliefs and social rules shared by a race of people in a place or time, their system of class, leadership and wealth

Discuss.

Important Vocabulary

Translate the vocabulary below and discuss each meaning.
Finally, write the word, mark the syllables and mark the stress with /.

1. culture _____

2. multicultural _____

3. racism _____

4. bias _____

5. prejudice _____

6. different customs _____

7. different beliefs _____

8. different practices _____

9. foreign _____

10. humanity _____

Celebrating with Verbs

decorating	watching	telling
making	baking	visiting
hanging	singing	buying
giving	getting	eating
writing	praying	cleaning

People in every culture have special times when they celebrate.

Celebrate means to have a special day or happy event.

1. Make a list of celebrations in your culture.

2. Write the date/s beside the celebration.

3. Read the verbs above and circle the 'ing' at the end.

4. Write 'yes' or 'no' to answer these questions.

a) Does your family decorate on any celebration? _____

b) Does your family buy anything special to celebrate? _____

c) Does your family cook or eat special food? _____

d) Is there a celebration that includes giving/getting? _____

5. What is your favorite celebration? _____

6. Why is it your favorite celebration?

_____

_____

Celebrations

My name is _____

People all over the world have celebrations. They celebrate different things for different reasons. It doesn't matter what religion or country or language you speak. Everyone has celebrations. Here are some of the ways that people might celebrate;

eating special foods   **praying**   **decorating**

singing   **visiting**   **having parties**

giving gifts   **having family get-togethers**   **inviting guests**

1. *What is the name of one of your celebrations ?*
   _____

2. *Circle the ways you celebrate that event.*

3. *What is the date of your celebration ?* _____

4. *Ask your parents questions to help you write about the meaning of your celebration, when it happens and what your family does. Use the back of this paper if you need to.*

   _____
   _____
   _____
   _____
   _____
   _____
   _____

5. *Attach a picture or photo about your celebration.*

   _____

The International Red Cross - Red Crescent

The Red Cross (Christian) Red Crescent (Muslim) Society always remains neutral in conflicts. That is why their personnel and vehicles are untouched and their workers are allowed access to treat the wounded, and to visit and to ensure basic needs are met for prisoners of war/others imprisoned.

In addition, the Society works with refugee and displaced persons, the reunification of family and location of missing persons and documentation. The Society also helps in times of disasters.

The Red Cross-Red Crescent Society represents compassion and humanity throughout the world. A major concept in this topic is that agreement and collaboration between countries does occur.

Contact your local Society ahead of time and arrange for a speaker or presenter for your students' age group. There are several divisions; International work and work within a community.

The history of how the society started and how it works in international spheres is relevant to everyone. The Society work goes far beyond Blood Clinics and courses in life-saving.

To begin;

- Ask students what they know about this vehicle. (ambulance, the Red Cross or Red Crescent)

- If necessary point out the siren, the Red Cross, and the Red Crescent. Answer questions.

- Talk about the Society's work with Blood Clinics
- Try to elicit information about international aid.

Teachers may be able to arrange several sessions, days apart for older students in order to discuss both in-country and international supports.

In any case try to arrange a new session on water safety before summer holidays.

A New Verb Tense

Past Tense	Continuous Past Tense
The simple past tense	A continuing action = was/were + ing
1. I worked at McDonalds.	I <u>was</u> work<u>ing</u> all day long.
2. You studied last night.	You were studying for 3 hours.
3. He felt happy.	He was feeling sad yesterday.
4. She played outside.	She was playing all afternoon.
5. The wind blew.	It was blowing me away.
6. We sang in the choir.	We were singing beautifully.
7. You went to the gym.	You were doing exercises.
8. They rode horses.	They were riding every week.

Write 10 sentences using this new continuous tense.

Another Past Tense

Use "was" or "were" and the verb with -ing.

> For example: was driving
> were sleeping

- 1. Steve and Peter _____ their bikes. (ride)

- 2. Maria _____ her money for her mother's birthday. (save)

- 3. Daniel _____ on the test. (cheat)

- 4. Sofia _____ too much. (talk)

- 5. My friend _____ to learn to play chess. (try)

Write a sentence for these verbs.

was watching _____.

were studying _____.

was driving _____.

were walking _____.

was flying _____.

was running _____.

Free Time Activities and Hobbies

Read these sports words. Underline the ones you have tried.
- Circle the ones you are good at.

jogging	rollerblading	cycling	skateboarding
bowling	horseback riding	golf	tennis
ping pong	darts	pool	karate
gymnastics	archery	boxing	wrestling
skydiving	baseball	football	weightlifting
basketball	volleyball	hiking	hockey
soccer	lacrosse	skating	sailing
surfing	swimming	scuba diving	snorkeling
fishing	waterskiing	rafting	snowmobiling

Read these hobby words. Underline the ones you have tried.
- Circle the ones you are good at.

sewing	knitting	pottery	painting
camping	coin collecting	model building	bird watching
exercising	photography	craft-making	walking
playing an instrument	stamp collecting	reading	writing
drawing	shopping		

What are some new sports or hobbies you would like to try?

_____

_____

Location Vocabulary

Location	Vocabulary
airport	restaurant
home	movie theatre
office	school
park	drug store
street	ice rink/ arena
beach	circus
jail	concert
jungle	underwater
doctor	dentist
museum	hospital
police station	farm
bakery	hair salon
gym/gymnasium	church
mosque	temple/synagogue
fire department	laundry room

Locations

Read the sentences. Then write the correct location.

1. I go in and sit down. Then I look at a menu and choose food. A waiter or waitress comes and asks me what I want. After, I have to pay. I am in a _____.

2. I wrote a letter and sent it to my cousin who lives in Canada. I had to buy a stamp at the _____.

3. My whole family goes out for a drive in the country on Sunday. We are looking for a place to pick apples. Then we see a sign and drive into the _____. We walk all around and pick the apples from the trees.

4. It's a very hot summer day. My family puts towels, a blanket and a picnic lunch in our car. Then we drive to water, unpack and walk on the sand, swim and have a barbeque. Yum -BBQ It's fun to be at the _____.

5. I need to get my hair cut. But first the lady needs to wash my hair. If I was a boy, I would go to a barber, but I'm a girl, so I go to the _____.

6. My aunt is coming to visit us from France so we'll go to the _____ to pick her up.

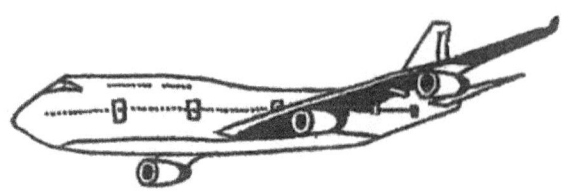

Where Does it Happen?

restaurant	beach	farm	gym	hotel
post office	grocery	store	school	bank
church / mosque / synagogue / temple				
hair salon	train station	hospital	street	airport
laundry room	home	park		office

Read the verbs and write the location.

1. sun tanning, swimming, floating _____
2. having tests, laying down, receiving surgery _____
3. buying a ticket, getting on, carrying your bags _____
4. swinging, sliding, relaxing, listening _____
5. buying, paying, licking, mailing _____
6. walking, watching, laughing, seeing _____
7. reserving, arriving, staying, sleeping, paying _____
8. walking, choosing, picking, putting, carrying _____
9. looking, ordering, waiting, eating, paying _____
10. reading, writing, talking, thinking, studying _____
11. running, stretching, jumping, exercising _____
12. sleeping, eating, relaxing, cleaning _____
13. kneeling, praying, singing, thinking _____
14. arriving, departing, lining up, flying _____
15. taking out, putting in, cashing, saving _____
16. looking, crossing, driving, walking _____
17. typing, sorting, filing, answering phones _____
18. washing, drying, sorting, folding, carrying _____
19. washing, drying, cutting, styling, paying _____
20. looking, selecting, shopping, buying, carrying _____

What Do You Like to Do?

1. Listen to the teacher pronounce each of the words.
2. Mark stress ' and divide into syllables / with the teacher's help.
3. Help each other translate or mime any words.
4. Circle the activities that you want to do after doing each section.

A. Water Activities
kayak   canoe   surf   water-ski   swim
scuba diving   snorkeling   sailing   fishing   skidoo

B. Ice Activities
skating   hockey   ice-fishing   curling
windsurfing   figure-skating

C. Ball Activities
baseball   basketball   soccer   tennis
volleyball   golf   football   ping-pong

D. Other Activities
gymnastics   cards   singing   biking   riding   arts   gamer

photography   dance   reading   movies   skateboarding

computer   badminton   music   hiking   tobogganing

camping   acting   snowboarding   traveling   cooking

Name
Survey Question

Who did you ask?	Answer

Surveys, Polls, Questionnaires and Interviews

In-class surveys, polls, questionnaires and interviews offer learners multiple opportunities to use the vocabulary, structures and discourse of any given topic. These tasks are considered to be low-risk activities since students won't be singled out - everyone else is speaking too.

Surveys, Polls and Questionnaires can be structured:
- ✓ to practise, review, gather and/or listen for specifics
- ✓ to generate discourse using new concepts and skills
- ✓ to obtain subjective experiences and opinions

Curriculum tasks can be adapted to this activity as well:
- ✓ by asking about motives, details, characters, thoughts
- ✓ by having students reply to True-False data/discourse
- ✓ have students decide on/prioritise issues/ideas gathered

Ways to Structure the Task

Opinions – What do you think . . . . . What are your thoughts . . .
Past Tenses – Why did . . . What happened . . .
Perfect Tenses – Have you . . . What sports/hobbies have you . . .
Vocabulary – Which words describe . . .
Explain, List reasons/details – Tell me how . . . Why . . .

Jobs

A. Read these words. Translate words you don't know.

actress   chef   driver   caretaker   pilot

waiter   teacher   singer   writer   painter

artist   carpenter   secretary   butcher   model

hairdresser   police officer   baker   dentist   plumber

pharmacist   lawyer   farmer   scientist   musician

computer programmer   mail carrier   salesclerk

B. What job would you like to do? _____.

What jobs have your parents done? _____.

_____

C. Who does these jobs?

1. typing, filing, answering phones _____.
2. styling, washing, cutting, shaping _____.
3. designing, sculpting, drawing, painting _____.
4. cutting, chopping, measuring, mixing, pouring _____.
5. planning, instructing, marking _____.
6. watching, checking, catching, guarding _____.
7. fixing, measuring, cutting, taking something off _____.
8. asking, carrying, putting, writing checks _____.
9. trying on, taking off, walking, posing _____.
10. practicing, playing, creating, carrying _____.

Thesaurus

In 1852, in England, Peter Roget had a strange hobby. He made lists of words. Then he categorized them. He grouped the words together if they had the same, or a similar, meaning.

Roget's list grew longer and longer. When he had 1,000 groups of words, he put the groups in alphabetical order and made a book. The book was called Roget's Thesaurus.

The Thesaurus

A long time ago, Peter Roget, a doctor in England, had a hobby. He liked to make lists of words. Then he grouped or categorized the words. He grouped the words together if they had the same or a similar meaning. These are called synonyms.

At the end of the group he listed the opposite meaning of the word (antonym). Roget's lists grew longer and longer because he used a dictionary to get as many related words as he could. All together, Roget listed 1,000 groups. His lists of words were put in alphabetical order and first published in 1852. It was titled Roget's Thesaurus.

Roget died in 1869, but his idea became very popular and many more editions of his book were developed over the years. Although a Thesaurus does not give a definition for words like a dictionary does, the book is very useful for improving your vocabulary and for making your ideas more interesting and precise.

Using A Thesaurus

Look up the following words in a thesaurus. Then write the related choices. At the end, write the opposite.

try _____

_____

save _____

_____

make _____

_____

say _____

_____

go _____

_____

1. On the back of this paper write five more verbs.
2. Look them up in the thesaurus and list similar words.

Idioms

Idioms are tricky - what it says is not what it means.

When the teacher says the idiom, make a picture in your mind. After that, listen to the teacher and learn the true meaning.

Idiom   Meaning

1. ants in your pants
2. raining cats and dogs
3. Talk to the hand.
4. blow your top
5. backseat driver
6. cut it out
7. all heart
8. all ears
9. not all there

Idioms

Idioms are special expressions that don't mean what they seem to say. If you don't understand an idiom, it sounds crazy. Here are some idioms. Do you know what they mean? Talk about the real meaning and write it beside the idiom. Finally, draw a picture to illustrate 4 idiotic idioms.

1. Keep your pants on. _____

2. Keep an eye out. _____

3. I have butterflies in my stomach. _____

4. It's raining cats and dogs. _____

5. The teacher lost his temper. _____

6. Don't bug me. _____

7. You're pulling my leg. _____

8. Take my word for it. _____

9. I'm broke. _____

10. We don't see eye to eye. _____

11. Over my dead body. _____

12. The movie gave me goosebumps. _____

Idioms

Idioms are special expressions that don't mean what they seem to say. If you don't understand an idiom, it sounds crazy. Here are some idioms. Do you know what they mean? Talk about the real meaning and write it beside the idiom. Finally, draw a picture to illustrate 4 idiotic idioms.

1. Keep your pants on. _____

2. Keep an eye out. _____

3. I have butterflies in my stomach. _____

4. It's raining cats and dogs. _____

5. The teacher lost his temper. _____

6. Don't bug me. _____

7. You're pulling my leg. _____

8. Take my word for it. _____

9. I'm broke. _____

10. We don't see eye to eye. _____

11. Over my dead body. _____

12. The movie gave me goosebumps. _____

Idioms – 2 Sessions

A. Listen as each sentence is spoken.
B. Guess the meanings.
C. Write the real meaning beside each idiom.
D. Draw a picture about one of the idioms on another paper.
E. Write the idiom on the back of the drawing.
F. Staple the idiom pictures into a booklet.

1. Take it easy.
2. I'm broke.
3. He lost his temper.
4. We don't see eye to eye.
5. The baby cried his eyes out.
6. You're driving me up a wall.
7. You must be nuts!
8. Take my word for it.
9. Quit beefing!
10. Keep an eye out.
11. You're pulling my leg.
12. It's raining cats and dogs.
13. She broke my heart.
14. Stop monkeying around.
15. Over my dead body.
16. Don't cry over spilt milk.
17. Don't put all your eggs in one basket.
18. Take a load off your feet.
19. Easy come, easy go.
20. He cracks me up.
21. He's crying his head off.
22. Give me a break, will you?
23. He's on cloud nine.
24. He's all butterfingers.
25. I have butterflies in my stomach.
26. Money burns a hole in my pocket.
27. That movie gave me goose bumps.
28. I'm feeling blue.

Teaching Verbs

BC TEAL Newsletter   Mary Meyers

Steven Pinker who looks like a rock star is actually a linguistics explorer. In an interview (discovermagazine.com/2007/sep), Pinker said, "I spent 20 years doing research on verbs because it seemed to me that they tapped into fundamental human concepts and cognitive framing - in other words, the stuff of thought." Indeed, verb knowledge, or the lack of it, can affect language acquisition at any age. In this article, I want to share with you some of the activities I've tried for different needs.

A) An SK teacher was eager to try out the many ideas and activities that we discussed for her Korean student who knew no English. At the end of the year, a brief assessment indicated that the little girl had learned basic English, but she was unable to point to or voice many simple pictures of verb actions, even with prompting. These suggestions work for all newcomers.

1. **Directed Teaching** - Make a big book of verbs/doing things. Students ought to work in groups of 3 or 4, and glue large, magazine pictures illustrating a verb onto regular construction paper. Group work allows for collaboration (talk and support). Bind the book and include at least one picture from each student. Read it to the whole class several times, and then have a language buddy read it with ELLs. If possible, have students say the verb in their own language. Use the Audio-Lingual approach (see, hear and say) plus patterned verb phrases.

2. **Focus on One** – a technique to build involvement and to elicit response from a particular student. Look directly at the child, say a command and try for a response. Example: Do you want to (pause) read a book, draw a picture, or build with the blocks? Eventually the child will respond on his/her own.

3. **Teach it Twice** – well actually more than twice with reviews. Introduce 'gym' verbs, 'library' verbs or 'trip' verbs before the class goes to each place. Keep up the Directed-Teaching on new verbs for any new topic such as seasons, outdoor activities/curriculum. Aka Stephen Krashen: Multiple Input and Output

4. **Acquire Little Readers with Patterned, Repetitive Sentences** - I can ride a

I can ride in a car, a train, a bus, etc.   Audio-Lingual

B) When I worked as an in-class ESL co-teacher of grade five and six students, my classroom teacher-partner and I concentrated on the knowledge of irregular past tense verbs because it was a common error in his students' written work. Student results on our simple pre-test (with prompts) were abysmal, so we started direct, explicit teaching and activities to address the issue. Lesson activities included:

1. **Whole class correction** of the pre-test using the past tenses in contexts

2. **Making a Big Book** from student artwork to show an action before and after

   e.g., drink – drank, drive – drove, grow – grew, sell - sold, draw – drew, etc.

3. **Guided Chart and Worksheet Activities Using Patterned Spelling**

   Use irregular past tense forms. i.e,

   grew, blew, threw, drew, knew and flew

   thought, bought, fought, caught

   'o' - lost, cost, forgot, sold, drove, wrote, spoke, broke, woke, rode

4. **MadLib Style Worksheets** – short stories where students created 1/2 page

   stories then partnered to fill in the verb blanks

   Use any subject content as context for verb use in context.

5. **Spelling Lists**

C) With greater maturation and accumulated skills, junior grade students naturally work with more cognitively challenging verbs used in content instruction, texts and tests. Cognitive Academic Language Learning/CALL includes instruction of 'concept' and 'cognition' verbs to prepare ELLs for success in 'Academic Literacy' as required in higher grades. Some ideas for teaching 'concept' verbs are as follows:

1. **Teach a specific 'academic concept' verb** such as classify, predict, assess, infer, and discuss. Elicit responses so students can practice what they have to 'do', plus they'll hear lots of answers and explanations using longer discourse.

2. **Teach, and process an English Function verb** and its related vocabulary.

e.g., Function Verb: Compare

   Related vocabulary: both, however, on the other hand, but, although, etc.

   Topics: 2 people, 2 sports, a beach and a park, house to apartment, restaurants

3. **Point out verbs and their related nouns.**

Mark the stressed syllables. This activity can also be used to review suffixes.

discuss – discussion	identify – identification	summarize – summary
state – statement	decide – decision	explain – explanation
argue – argument	compare – comparison	achieve – achievement
create – creation	arrange – arrangement	evolve – evolution

4. **Bring attention to verbs with same spelling nouns.**

e.g., list (verb) – list (noun)

a. <u>List</u> the reasons why . . .   b. Make <u>a list</u> of . . .

survey – survey   support – support   plot – plot   record – record

Website Supports for Elementary Teachers

The following sites are deemed particularly useful. Add your own notes on the lines.

1. Language, Literacy Skills, Math - Worksheets and Ideas

The Internet Picture Dictionary - http://pdictionary.com/
A completely free, online multilingual picture dictionary designed especially for ESL students and beginning English. All ages

___

Education.com - https://www.education.com/
Lots of reproducible freebies. You have to search but there is a plethora of materials. I went to 'writing details personal narratives' and picked from there, since I'm doing some on-line tutoring.

___

http://www.kizclub.com/stories.htm
This is a fabulous site with so many worksheets, links, great printouts for students to retell classic stories, poems, etc. mini-book activities. Wow!

___

https://www.allkidsnetwork.com/

___

http://www.esl-galaxy.com/

___

https://ca.ixl.com/ela

___

http://www.toolsforeducators.com

http://www.enchantedlearning.com/Home.html

http://www.sheppardsoftware.com

2. Read Aloud Storybooks that are Easy to Set Up

www.justbooksreadaloud.com

Indianapolis Public Library www.indypl.org/readytoread/?p=6150

Books Read Aloud for Children Website – so many book series
https://www.youtube.com/channel/UCVRxOtQqiFoWEaQ_uTKe4jw/videos

Reading Pioneers - Dr. Seuss, Curious George, Arthur Series etc.
https://www.youtube.com/channel/UC42UhuU_wJt10pNX5Q-xplg/videos

Books Read Aloud for Children Website - so many book series
https://www.youtube.com/channel/UCVRxOtQqiFoWEaQ_uTKe4jw/videos

---

Reading Pioneers - Dr. Seuss, Curious George, Arthur Series etc.
https://www.youtube.com/channel/UC42UhuU_wJt10pNX5Q-xplg/videos

---

Sites for Curriculum Instruction and Messages

3. Translations for Students or Parents

translate.google.com

http://translate.reference.com

www.microsofttranslator.com

What's Next ?

Students practice speaking and listening to new vocabulary.
* Partners place a barrier between them, perhaps a file folder, or an open book.
* Each student gets copies of the same picture cards. Use 8+ cards such as school objects, animals or 18 opposites, etc.

One students starts the game by choosing one of his/her cards and saying the name of it. The partner listens, then locates that card on his/her side of the barrier and places it as the first in a row on his/her desk. This continues until all the cards are called.

Finally, the partners lift the barrier and check to see if they are lined up the same.

Use the following picture pages to play What's Next'.

Set 1

Set 3

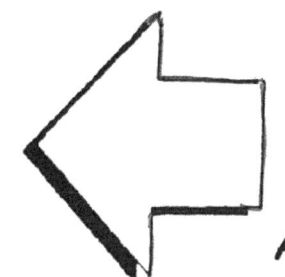 # Before and After
A simple dimple thinking game

Share the intriguing visual book 'Before After' 2014, Candlewick Press (available at the library). It's wordless and simply shows things before and after: an acorn then a tree, night then day, caterpillar then butterfly, sheep then wool, a pile of bricks then a brick wall, cow then ice cream, etc. If you/librarian can't locate the book, make your own pictures.

Two ways to play

1. The day after sharing the book, have students get in partners or small groups and think up ideas for before and after. One student from each group goes to the whiteboard and draws their best 'before' picture. The other groups guess the 'after'. The group with the right answer gets a point.

2. Relate the concept to verbs.
Have students illustrate a before and after picture on the front and back of a large piece of paper.

Show students your own examples such as:
- a child wears a bathing suit and then on the reverse side, the child is swimming in a pool or at the beach
- a boy falls off his bike then on the reverse, he cries/bleeds
- picking an apple, then eating it
- raining then someone splashing in a puddle
- throwing a ball then someone hits it with a bat

See examples next page

She drinks the juice.

She drank the juice.

Draw Drew

First   second   next   now   then   after
after that   afterwards   when that is done   at last

Use the words to tell the sequence.

One Saturday morning ….

Then …

After that ….

At last …..

Next …

Finally …

Fairy Tale Manipulatives

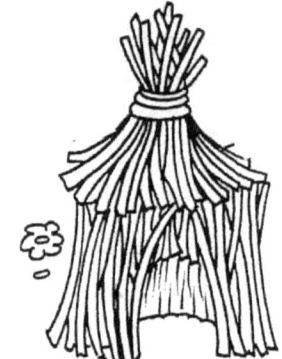

Students color then cut around the pictures. They listen to the story re-telling and move the characters forward as each is involved.

Most manipulatives can be purchased from TeachersPayTeachers.com – write what you want in their search bar. There are many freebies in addition to to inexpensive resources on this site.

This book also has a list of other websites to print out free resources.

Story-Telling and Story Maps

Tell and re-tell a story or song using contextual clues, pictures or manipulative objects. Students will follow along as they listen, review and learn vocabulary and sentence structure. Add more details and description with each re-telling.

Steps

1. Choose an easy and fairly short story to read and re-tell.
   For example, The Gingerbread Man, Old MacDonald
   Use a book with large pictures or even a video to begin.

2. Plan to re-tell with either manipulatives or a story map.
   a) See an example of a story map at the bottom of this page.

   b) Manipulatives may be
      - paper objects that students color and cut out
        (See example 'I know an Old Lady Who Swallowed a Fly')
      - sets of characters and related items copied from a book
      - plasticene or clay figures and objects that students make
      - puzzle pieces of a story (i.e., Kdgn board puzzles)

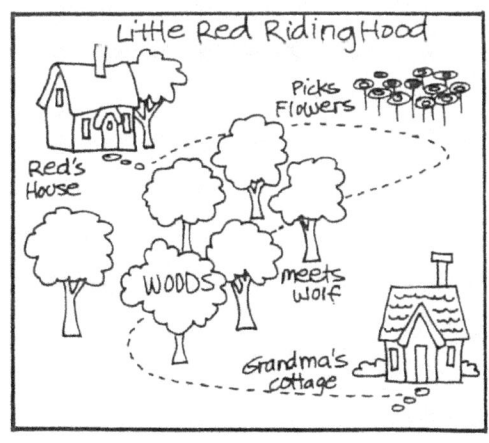

Red Riding Hood

After introducing the story and vocabulary in a picture book, the teacher retells the story as students bring the character card in line on their desks.

basket of food

sick grandmother

forest   big bad wolf   grandma's house

big eyes, big ears
big teeth   woodman   The wolf is dead

Speak Out

Small Group Game – Speaking Practice

Students take turns, picking up the top card and saying something about the topic (use for opinions/details/curriculum questions/discourse). Enlarge this form and make multiple copies on colored stock card, then place in a baggie.

Sequence a Poem

Use the following rhyming poem as a listening activity about animals.

- The teacher says the poem to the class with intonation and gestures. Perhaps it can be displayed on a whiteboard.

- The teacher hands out copies of the poem and this time reads it. Students name and color the animal that is being named.

- Later, the teacher hands out sets of the poem to student partners. The poem is cut into strips.
  * Hint – choose only 8-10 sections of the poem.

- As the poem is read, students locate the correct strip and place it first in a row on their desk.

- Students might want to repeat a part of the poem.

- Students might like to perform a skit with the poem, or even show it off at an assembly.

Every day, when I went to school,
or out to play,
my mother would say,

See you later, alligator.

 After a while, crocodile.

Pretty soon, raccoon.

 Bye, bye, butterfly.

Time to go, buffalo.

 Take care, teddy bear.

Out the door, dinosaur.

 Gotta flee, honeybee.

So long for now, baby cow.

 Good luck, yellow duck.

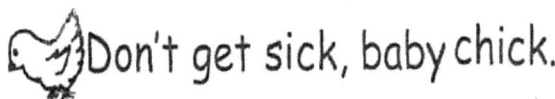Don't get sick, baby chick.

Miss you too, kangaroo.

Don't laugh, yellow giraffe.

Scat, scat,  pussycat.

Time to embark, baby shark.

What's the deal, baby seal?

Stay outta jail, baby whale.

You're kind of funny, baby bunny.

Hit the road, bumpy toad.

Don't be late, rattlesnake.

Blow a kiss, tuna fish.

 Hang loose, silly goose.

Stop your cryin', little lion.

What's the drama, furry llama?

 Gotta scram, little lamb.

Get in line, porcupine.

 Stay sweet, my parakeet.

Yes, of course, pretty horse.

 Outta the house, little mouse.

Not another word, blue bird.

 If you wanna, iguana.

Look at us, octopus.

Give a hug ladybug.

Gotta go, kiddo.

Take care.

Bye bye.

Fooled You – 1 Session
Following Directions, Body Vocabulary

These are balancing tricks by Nancy Harvey.

Hopeless Hopper
Trick – There's no way students will be able to hop

First, ask the students to hop. Then tell them you will make it impossible for them to hop. Let 1 student try it first, and after that they can all try.
Tell the student to bend over and grab his toes. Gravity prevents them from hopping. They'll fall over.

Tiptoe Trap

Students will do this trick against a door, so make sure no one is coming in or going out. Hold the door so it doesn't bump into them. Ask students to stand up on their toes. Then choose 1 student to put their feet on either side of the door, with their stomach and nose touching the edge. Ask the student to stand on his/her toes. Then ask the student if his toes are glued to the floor.

Sticky Foot

You will stick the student's foot to the floor. Ask one student to stand sideways with one side of his body against the wall. Make sure that the student is touching the wall with his cheek, arm and foot. Then ask the student to lift up the other foot – the one farthest away from the wall. It will be impossible to do – because of balance.

Would You Rather?

Would you rather questions are a great way for students to get to know each other or to start conversations by just asking "why" after a 'would you rather' question. It's a perfect opportunity for students to meet others and learn about them, and perhaps, even make a new friend.

You'll need multiple sets of 'Would you rather...' questions. It's best if the cards are printed on card-stock, which is heavier than paper. Cut them out and place the sets in a baggies.

In a small group, students shuffle the cards and place them face down. They take turns choosing a 'would you rather' question and asking each member of the group. If it's just partners, both students can answer the question.

Young students and beginners will probably answer with one word, but the teacher could take up some of the questions after the game to expand the language exercise.

Copy the following pages and cut and separate the questions.

Would you rather have a cat or a dog?

Would you rather live at the beach or on a mountain?

Would you rather drive a motorcycle or a fancy car?

Would you rather be smart or rich?

Would you rather watch a movie or a music video?

Would you rather be athletic (sporty) or artistic?

Would you rather have a different color of eyes?

Would you rather have friends or pets?

Would you rather eat lunch at school or at home?

Would you rather have gym or art?

Would you rather be funny or interesting?

Would you rather be a singer, a dancer or an actor?

Would you rather have pizza or hamburgers and fries?

Would you rather skate or ski or swim or sail?

Teacher Information for Verbs of State

In English grammar, a *stative verb* is a verb used to describe a state of being (I *am*) or situation (I *have*). It's how something **is**, **feels**, or **appears**. These verbs don't show physical action (I *run*) Stative verbs can describe a mental or emotional state of being (I *doubt*) as well as a physical state (Peter *was* here).

Verbs that express a state rather than an action usually relate to thoughts, emotions, relationships, senses, and states of being. Common examples include *be, have, like, seem, prefer, understand, belong, doubt, hate,* and *know*.

Senses and perception verbs include data coming into your five senses:

- See Hear Smell Taste See

Emotion and thought verbs include:

- Love Hate Adore Like Despise Doubt Feel Believe Forget Remember Agree
- Enjoy Need Think Recognize Prefer Understand Suspect Appear

Possession verbs include:

- Have Belong Include Own Want

Verbs that describe states of being include:

- Be/Are/Is Weigh Contain Involve Consist

Teachers ought to introduce this concept in a simple, direct way. The main idea is for students to understand that they are verbs. Students do not need to memorize the definition. Following is a student activity to identify the verb.

Underline the Verbs.   Name _____

1. I know the answer. You don't.   (don't = do not)

2. She needs her mother because she feels really sick.

3. I want a cookie but I hate that kind.

4. I think it's Monday, but I am not sure.   (I am = I'm)

5. Yes, we like TV shows, but we love movies more.

6. I think he lied, and I believe you.

7. Please taste this for me. It might be too spicy.

8. I smell smoke. Do you?

9. He only has enough money for a hamburger.

10. I understand the question, but it confuses me.

11. I hate eggs. They are gross.   (They are = They're)

12. I remember now. I agree with you that the accident was his fault.

13. I am really tired. I need a nap.

14. Who owns the red car? I do.

15. They weighed me in the doctor's office. I look skinny, but I am strong.

16. He wants a truck not a car. I forget which kind.

17. This dog belongs to that guy. He owns it.

Verbs as Cognitive Processes

In junior grades, learning becomes more challenging for students in terms of cognitive processing. This expectation is reflected in the use of verbs that require specific thinking skills.

compare
summarize
identify
discuss
predict
infer
adapt
describe
prioritize
analyze
decide
provide arguments for/against

Compare Summer Words

hotel and a motel

a snorkel and SCUBA

a lake and a river

a beach and a pool

a tent and a trailer

a park and a beach

a suntan and a sunburn

a holiday and a camp

contrast

Definition

to tell the differences between 2 things

Contrast these
WalMart – School

Polar bear – Panda bear

| but   however   although   is – isn't |

Verbs into Nouns

1. Listen to the pronunciation of each verb and noun. Repeat each noun.
2. Mark the 'stress' syllable with the teacher's help.

1. decide   decision

2. compare   comparison

3. discuss   discussion

4. think   thought

5. prove   proof

6. summarize   summary

7. respond   response

8. achieve   achievement

9. argue   argument

10. state   statement

Teaching Verbs

BC TEAL Newsletter   Mary Meyers

Steven Pinker who looks like a rock star is actually a linguistics explorer. In an interview (discovermagazine.com/2007/sep), Pinker said, "I spent 20 years doing research on verbs because it seemed to me that they tapped into fundamental human concepts and cognitive framing - in other words, the stuff of thought." Indeed, verb knowledge, or the lack of it, can affect language acquisition at any age. In this article, I want to share with you some of the activities I've tried for different needs.

A) An SK teacher was eager to try out the many ideas and activities that we discussed for her Korean student who knew no English. At the end of the year, a brief assessment indicated that the little girl had learned basic English, but she was unable to point to or voice many simple pictures of verb actions, even with prompting. These suggestions work for all newcomers.

1. **Directed Teaching** - Make a big book of verbs/doing things. Students ought to work in groups of 3 or 4, and glue large, magazine pictures illustrating a verb onto regular construction paper. Group work allows for collaboration (talk and support). Bind the book and include at least one picture from each student. Read it to the whole class several times, and then have a language buddy read it with ELLs. If possible, have students say the verb in their own language. Use the Audio-Lingual approach (see, hear and say) plus patterned verb phrases.

2. **Focus on One** – a technique to build involvement and to elicit response from a particular student. Look directly at the child, say a command and try for a response. Example: Do you want to (pause) read a book, draw a picture, or build with the blocks? Eventually the child will respond on his/her own.

3. **Teach it Twice** – well actually more than twice with reviews. Introduce 'gym' verbs, 'library' verbs or 'trip' verbs before the class goes to each place. Keep up the Directed-Teaching on new verbs for any new topic such as seasons, outdoor activities/curriculum. Aka Stephen Krashen: Multiple Input and Output

4. **Acquire Little Readers with Patterned, Repetitive Sentences** - I can ride a

I can ride in a car, a train, a bus, etc.   Audio-Lingual

B) When I worked as an in-class ESL co-teacher of grade five and six students, my classroom teacher-partner and I concentrated on the knowledge of irregular past tense verbs because it was a common error in his students' written work. Student results on our simple pre-test (with prompts) were abysmal, so we started direct, explicit teaching and activities to address the issue. Lesson activities included:

1. **Whole class correction** of the pre-test using the past tenses in contexts

2. **Making a Big Book** from student artwork to show an action before and after

e.g., drink – drank, drive – drove, grow – grew, sell - sold, draw – drew, etc.

3. **Guided Chart and Worksheet Activities Using Patterned Spelling**

   Use irregular past tense forms. i.e,

   grew, blew, threw, drew, knew and flew

   thought, bought, fought, caught

   'o' - lost, cost, forgot, sold, drove, wrote, spoke, broke, woke, rode

4. **MadLib Style Worksheets** – short stories where students created 1/2 page

   stories then partnered to fill in the verb blanks

   Use any subject content as context for verb use in context.

5. **Spelling Lists**

C) With greater maturation and accumulated skills, junior grade students naturally work with more cognitively challenging verbs used in content instruction, texts and tests. Cognitive Academic Language Learning/CALL includes instruction of 'concept' and 'cognition' verbs to prepare ELLs for success in 'Academic Literacy' as required in higher grades. Some ideas for teaching 'concept' verbs are as follows:

1. **Teach a specific 'academic concept' verb** such as classify, predict, assess, infer, and discuss. Elicit responses so students can practice what they have to 'do', plus they'll hear lots of answers and explanations using longer discourse.

2. **Teach, and process an English Function verb** and its related vocabulary.

e.g., Function Verb: Compare

    Related vocabulary: both, however, on the other hand, but, although, etc.

    Topics: 2 people, 2 sports, a beach and a park, house to apartment, restaurants

3. **Point out verbs and their related nouns.**

Mark the stressed syllables. This activity can also be used to review suffixes.

discuss – discussion	identify – identification	summarize – summary
state – statement	decide – decision	explain – explanation
argue – argument	compare – comparison	achieve – achievement
create – creation	arrange – arrangement	evolve – evolution

4. **Bring attention to verbs with same spelling nouns.**

e.g., list (verb) – list (noun)

a. <u>List</u> the reasons why . . .   b. Make <u>a list</u> of . . .

survey – survey   support – support   plot – plot   record – record

WatchKnowLearn.org

Okay, this is not a game – but I just had to add it in case you weren't aware of it. WatchKnowLearn is a super-directory of over 50,000 free educational video links that are organized by subject matter.

You'll have to sign up on their website even though the service is free for teachers, parents and students everywhere.

Everything on the site can be translated into Spanish or Chinese by clicking the language button at the top right.

Rather than spend a lot of time clicking on the various subject areas, I went to the Search bar and typed in Compound Words first and then later I searched for Persuasive Techniques. Both times I was pleased with the range and quality of offerings. A great many had animation with text and voice or song overlay – all of which is attractive and fun for younger students. Why turn yourself upside down to get attention – just try a pertinent video.

www.ingramcontent.com/pod-product-compliance
Lightning Source LLC
Chambersburg PA
CBHW081253040426
42453CB00014B/2391